Dance with a Purpose

Dancing in the church or
Dancing in God's presence

by SABRINA McKENZIE

Jamarl Publishing
www.sabrinamckenzie.org

Dance with a Purpose
ISBN 0-9719818-2-5
© 2005 by Sabrina McKenzie
Decatur, GA 30035

Published by Jamarl Publishing
Decatur, GA 30035

Printed in the United States of America.

This book is dedicated to my mom,
Thelma Taylor,
for s t r e t c h i n g me
and letting me know
that I could do all things.

Dance without Christ is exercise,
but dancing in Christ is
"Dance with a Purpose".

— *Sabrina McKenzie*

Dancing in the church or
Dancing in God's presence

Acknowledgements

I would like to take this opportunity to thank some special people who have sacrificed time and time again to allow me to walk in the ministry God created for me.

— To my husband, Kenneth McKenzie, I send my love and appreciation. To my three beautiful children: Anadi, Khidhar, and Imani McKenzie for allowing me to spend time away from you as I serve in ministry.

— To my Pastor, Bishop Eddie L. Long, Elder Vanessa Long, and the New Birth Family for giving me a space to grow.

— To Kevin Bond and the entire New Birth Liturgical Dance Team who co-labor with me in this ministry.

— To Chiquita Lockley — This book would not have been completed without your help.

— And a very special thanks to all my haters that became my motivators.

— And finally, to my heavenly Father who knew His plans for me and choreographed my steps to create the dance I call *purpose and destiny*. I am forever indebted to you.

Introduction

Before you read one thing in this book, please know that dance ministry is a lifestyle. This book will not teach you how to dance better or how to move the crowd, however, it *will* instruct you on simple principles of worship as a lifestyle. This book is geared toward anyone in the Worship & Arts ministry. It speaks to your first call as a worshipper.

The words in this book will help you understand your role as a Priest and Levite. The word *Levite* stems from the root word *Levi*. Levi was Rachel's third son. Because she wanted her husband Jacob to love her, she bore many sons for him. Levi means "attached". Her desire was that as a result of this son Levi, her husband would feel more attached to her.

The things that take place in the natural are merely a reflection of what God has done in the Spirit realm. God is our husband, and he gave his son Jesus so that we could become attached to him. No man enters into the Kingdom unless they come through the door of Christ. Jesus has become our high Priest and our gateway to salvation. In him we live, move, and have our being.

In order to sing and dance in a holy dimension, we must be attached to God through Christ. We must become the gateway for the lost. We are Christ's representatives on earth. Levites are ambassadors of the Kingdom of God, and we are attached to him through the blood of Christ. The world and the church should see Christ when they look at our lifestyles. The manner in which we live should make those who meet us want to serve our God. You are the bridge for the lost! Worship is not something we do, but instead it is actually the condition of your heart. From the abundance of your heart your mouth will speak. Wash your heart with the Word of God so that you may become a part of the Levitical tribe.

Each week in congregations around the world praise songs and dances take place. Worship services have become so predictable and structured that we now have a set time in the program to sing and a set time to dance. The service is not open for corporate worship or prophetic utterances because everything is so well rehearsed. Our psalmists have become superstars not singing for less than a few thousand. Many pastors are glamorized pimps, *show me the money,* and our dance ministers are living lifestyles contrary to the word of God. We have everything in church except God.

We place a symbol of Christianity on the building, but we leave out Christ. We spend 10 minutes in song and the rest of the program is spent on announcements, greetings, and the pastor's scripted message. And please do not forget the offering!

But where is God? Have you invited Him? Are there miracles taking place in your church? Is healing going forth consistently? Is there an over-flow of deliverance? When is the last time you ministered and the alter was filled with unbelievers surrendering their lives to Christ? Who is making a resting place of habitation for Jesus? Is your church a house of prayer and worship? When your worship leader sings, are you left bowing in the presence of God or are you just hyped waiting on the next show? Those who worship God must worship Him in spirit and in truth.

The reason the church has become so powerless in the world is because the fullness of worship has not been restored. **ACTS 15:16** states, *"After this I will return, and will build again the tabernacle of David, which is fallen down; and I will build again the ruins thereof, and I will set it up"*. God chose worshippers for the highest position in Israel. **PROVERBS 8:17** states, *"I love them that love me; and those that seek me early shall find me"*.

This word is simple. It points back to Jesus and deals with the restoration of the arts as true kings, priests, and worshippers loving Jesus and seeking Jesus. It expounds on the very purpose and power of worship and dance. It is from these lines of questions regarding the state of worship in the church today that prompted me to write this book. It is my sincere prayer and desire that the information shared in these next several pages will convict you to re-evaluate your call and begin to take the ministry of Worship & Arts more seriously.

What is a Dance Minister?

A dance minister is a person who answered the call from God to dance. There are several types of dance ministers within the apostle, prophet, evangelist, pastor, and teacher five-fold ministry; however, there are a few requirements they all should have. Namely, a dance minister: {1} must understand righteousness {**ROMANS 10:3**}; {2} must be broken {**PSALM 51:16-17**}; {3} must belong to a local church; and {4} must be a worshipper {**JOHN 4:23**}.

A liturgical dance minister follows the liturgical order. Liturgical comes from the root word liturgy. The liturgy is the public work or service of God by which Christ continues the redemption through the Church. The liturgical dance can only operate inside and outside the church. This type dance observes the ordinances set by the church: such as Holy Communion, the Resurrection, Christmas, etc.

CHAPTER 1

The call to dance

When I was 12 years old, I received my call to ministry. I did not see any lightening bolts. There was no angel that sat on my bed, and I did not hear a physical voice of God; however, I just knew he was speaking to me. I had a yearning desire to confess my sins to him and, at that moment, he affirmed me.

I was so excited and overjoyed that I wanted to share this goodness with everyone. Even though I was not ready to fully commit my life, I knew I had been chosen. At the time I did not know about the ministry gifts or the call to dance. I just knew that God was going to do something very special with my life, and he wanted me to preach His word.

I really did not see a display of dancing in the church. I was raised in a Pentecostal church and there was no dancing. In fact, dancing was considered a sin. This was the main reason I did not want to be saved because I thought that I would have to give up my love for dancing altogether. After my brother died of aids and my sister was murdered, I knew that the Lord was after me. I had been running from His call on my life for ten years, and now it was time to answer. The Holy Spirit led me to the first chapter of Jonah where the Lord told him to go to Nineveh to preach, but because Jonah disobeyed the call of God on his life, he was swallowed by the whale. Well, I knew if I continued to put off His call on my life that I would surely die early.

You see, I was still in the world and the world was very much in me. As a native of New York City, there was always a party to go to and a dance battle on the floor. Every weekend my girl friends and I would head to the Latin Quarters or Union Square to get our groove on. I danced in several music videos for artists such as TLC, Monie Love, Joe and Dallas Austin's group, the Highland Place Mobsters. I even toured with several famous entertainers, so I just knew I was going to make it big as a dancer. I tried to bargain with the Lord. This is what I said: "You see Lord, if you let me make it big by dancing, then I can buy my mother a house, and she will never have to work again. When I turn 50, I will give my life to you and stop dancing." I wanted to strike a deal with God because I really could not fathom never dancing again. I loved to dance! Every Saturday morning my mother would make us get up to clean the house but instead of cleaning, I would be dancing in the mirror. When I turned 16, I took my allowance and paid to attend dance classes. In high school I joined the dance team. In college I joined the dance team. Everywhere I went I wanted to dance. Looking back at everything now, it seems easy to say that my destiny would be tied into dancing but I never had a clue I would be dancing for the Lord.

When I finally surrendered my life to the Lord in 1993, I left the entertainment business completely. I was told that dancing was pleasurable and a sin before God, so I put down my dancing shoes and asked the Lord what he wanted me to do. Well, after three years of sitting my gift on the shelf, I saw dancing one day in church. I was attending a Sunday service and I saw a young lady dancing to Kirk Franklin's *Silver and Gold*. First of all that was my favorite song! Secondly, I could not believe that she was dancing. My eyes lit up and I began to weep. Following her every movement, my body began to sway. I no longer saw her, but I saw myself. You see, I had already married the song because that was my personal testimony. I would rather have Jesus than silver and gold. I wept the entire song and dance. When service was over, I ran to the dance ministry to find out the date of the next rehearsal. I was so hungry for the ministry of dance.

For the next several months, and even years, I tried in vain to find workshops and conferences pertaining to dance. For three years the Lord had my gift on the shelf so that he could sanctify it. Could you imagine dancing in the clubs one day and getting saved the next day and dancing in the church the day after? No. There had to be a period of *wait* and *sanctification*. I had to sanctify myself so that I could present my body as a living sacrifice. Salvation comes with the confession of the mouth and heart; however, worship is a lifestyle. If I had danced the day after I gave my life to Christ, I would have perverted the sanctuary because the dance I knew was not holy. I was filled with songs like Bobby Brown's *Tender Roni* and Salt and Pepa's *I Am Independent.*

When you are a babe in Christ, you should first spend time with the father renewing your mind. You need to take time out to allow God to renew your mind and wash your mind with His word. Those secular songs had shaped my mind and gripped my life. During my period of sanctification, God was making me over again.

If you look at the life of David, the day that he was anointed was not the same day that he became king. He went back into the field and continued to work. Jesus was also in the temple at age 12, but he did not begin His ministry until he was 30 years old. Joseph was called at an early age too; however, it took years of grooming before he reigned as king. You will likely feel like Joseph once you realize that the Lord has called you, but before you can put on your crown and share this news with everyone, He requires that you wait and allow His process to manifest in your life. God's manifestation will speak louder than your justification. The Lord's call is often times a prelude to what you will become. Remember, he knows where you are and where you're going. Jeremiah 29:11 declares, "I know the plans I have for you." The Lord knows your very thoughts, and He has ordained you before you were formed in your mother's womb. He knew when you would back slide, fall short and even reject him, and yet he still called you.

If you have to ask, "Have I been called," then you have not been called to that particular assignment. You will know when the Lord summons you. It almost feels like a Paul experience on the road to Damascus. At the appointed time, the Lord will pluck you out of your sin and call you to himself. You did not choose the Lord; he chose you. I am willing to submit that whatever your passion is, whatever your gifts are, and whatever you love to do, the Lord has called you to do that very assignment. It is almost offensive not to answer the call. Just think about it. If you called a friend on the phone and he or she picked up but never responded, would you be offended?

Stop having foreplay with the Lord and become intimate with Him. He wants to use you and your gift. Yes, I ran this game too: I'd say, "Okay Lord, when I clean myself up, then I will surrender my life to you." If you could clean up your life on your own, you would have already done so. You can't do it in your own strength. You need the Holy Spirit to lead and guide you. If you answer your call then the Lord will help you through the process of a NEW LIFE. You don't have to focus on how to live holy enough for service. Just continue to walk with him and he will guide you into the path of righteousness for His namesake.

Just because you were a ballerina in the world does not mean you were called to the dance ministry. Just because you can kick past your head and split on the floor does not mean you have been called to dance. And just because you created the best choreography when you were in the world does not mean you can use that same choreography in the church.

I know you are saying, "But you just said that whatever you are passionate about, that is a part of your call." Yes exactly! But it is not complete. Take time out to consecrate yourself. Cry out to the Lord and ask him, "God what would you have me do?" Yield yourself to him as a willing vessel. Turn down your plate by fasting. Don't answer your telephone and get in His word. There are several calls in the dance ministry. You could be called to lead intercessory prayer through dance. Maybe God has given you a vision to make holy garments. Maybe God has called you to evangelize in the dance. Ask God. He is your maker and your creator. He said in His word that the deep calls to the deep. He is calling you by His spirit. Quiet yourself so that you can hear him. If you have a holy passion, it was inspired by God. Too many dance ministries make the mistake of placing the best dancer as the dance ministry leader, and then people wonder why there is so much hell in the ministry. That person has been placed there by people, and not by God. Who man appoints, man can remove, but whoever God appoints, no devil in hell can shake. Pray and ask God, "What is my assignment? What should I do in the ministry of dance? Or even better, do I belong in the ministry of dance?"

Leaders, pray and ask God who should lead the dance ministry. It is not the most popular, best looking, most experienced, best technique or pastor's daughter that God is looking for. God is looking at the heart and oftentimes man is taken by the outward expressions. If you have already experienced this, then can I get an Amen? And if you have not experienced this use of respect of person, then try these few examples to find the true heart of your dance ministers.

- For the person that has the best techniques and most experience, only give him/her a flag to use during the choreography. If s/he has to be in the front and gets upset when placed on the sides or back, this person is not ready to lead.
- For the person that has been following you every-where because s/he wants to assist you, tell them you are considering someone else as your armor bearer. If s/he gets upset, that person is not called to lead at that time.
- For the person who always has an opinion and is very good at choreography, tell him/her to lead dance at 5:00 am intercessory prayer. It's likely that s/he will make up every excuse in the world saying they have been called to dance, not to intercessory prayer. News flash: **If you have not been called to pray, then you are not called of God.** God is calling you for His service and for His use. You have to enter in like a child, which is sometimes hard to do when you feel like you have so much experience. I am challenging you to surrender your toe shoes to God. Surrender your modern dance to God. Surrender your marriage to God. Surrender your heart to God, and surrender your gifts in the ministry to God.

Please listen. You may be in a place where God has transitioned you to a new church or ministry, and the dance ministers there are novices. Maybe God is calling you to be submissive to <u>all</u> authority. There may be a situation where you may be an excellent dancer, but you are not the leader for the church's dance ministry. Perhaps God is calling you to be patient. Another scenario is that you may be the leader, but now your dance ministry has been sat down or placed on sabbatical. Maybe God is calling you to be humble. These are all characteristics of God, and he is constantly growing us in the fruits of His spirit. You must remember to yield yourself to Him and His ways. Become pliable like a child. You cannot say God has called you while you are still acting like the devil. Consecrate yourself. When you go through tragedies such as divorce, death, illness, and church transition, stop, go back to the Father, and ask Him what He is calling you to do. Some dance ministers are so stuck on their last call as apostle, pastor, or prophet that they miss their first call as servant and ambassador. You can only be an ambassador and serve when your life reflects His ways, with His primary charge being *if you love me, then you will keep my commandments.* My question to you is do you know who is calling you?

If you recognize that God has called you, did you answer His call? There are many of you who are operating in fear or procrastination. God told you to join the dance ministry, but after saying okay, you said "when I lose weight" or "when my schedule permits" or "God, please show me another sign". After a few contemplations you finally join, but *obedience* is doing what God says *when* he says to do it — not half way. Now you are in the dance ministry, and God told you to write a book. Here you are waiting, waiting and waiting. You are collecting other people's books. You are procrastinating by saying I don't have the time because I AM SO BUSY DOING YOUR MINISTRY God, or you are just too lazy to discipline yourself and pick up the pen. Yet, the Lord says, "If you sit down and write I will give you the words and the inspiration." I am really sharing my personal experiences with you. That's why I can tell you how you feel. The scariest part is that if you were to die right now, would you have completed your assignment? Do you want to hear "Well done thy good and faithful servant"?

Let's reflect on the parable about the three men with talents {**MATT 25:21-29**}. He who received five talents went and traded with them and received five more and likewise he that received two talents gained two more also. But he that received one dug it in the ground. Now the Lord says to the one with the five talents "Well done, good and faithful servant; you were faithful over a few things, I will make you ruler over many things. Enter into the joy of your Lord." Then the Lord spoke to the one with two talents. "Well done, good and faithful servant; you have been faithful over a few things, I will make you ruler over many things. Enter into the joy of your Lord." The third man said to God, "Lord, I knew you to be a hard man, reaping where you have not sown, and gathering where you have not scattered seed and I was afraid, and went and hid your talent in the ground. Look, there you have what is yours", but His Lord answered and said to him, "You wicked and lazy servant, you knew that I reap where I have not sown, and gather where I have not scattered seed. So you ought to have deposited my money with the bankers, and at my coming I would have received back my own with interest. Therefore take the talent from him, and give it to him who has ten talents. For to everyone who has, more will be given, and he will have abundance; but from him who does not have, even what he has will be taken away".

God has given you gifts according to the potential he placed inside of you. When you procrastinate, wait, or bury your talents, the Bible says God will **cast the unprofitable servant into the outer darkness.** There will be weeping and gnashing of teeth. Most people think, "Wow, now I'm saved. I made it into the Kingdom", but the Kingdom is realizing and manifesting your full potential. You were placed here with purpose and destiny on your life, and no one can carry out the assignment the Lord has designated for you. So when you wait or bury the gift, you are telling God that he made a mistake in choosing you, to which He will say: **Cast the unprofitable servant into the outer darkness.**

Repent to the Father and get busy about your father's business. Answer your many calls to be a mom, dad, entrepreneur, king and priest. Once you begin to unlock one gift, many others will be revealed. You will go from wanting to dance, to having visions about choreography that your body cannot perform, to stage plays, to dreaming about holy garments. If it seems much bigger than you and your limitations, Great! That means it must be God. He will exceed your visions and expectations and then equip you with the ability to do them through Him. You are a spiritual being having a human experience. I know you can do it because *greater is he that lives in you then he that is in the world* {**1 JOHN 4:4**}. The greater one lives in you. You have an advocate in the Holy Spirit. The Lord is right now making intercessions on your behalf, and the angels will guide you through your assignment. You MUST answer the call!

CHAPTER 2

The cost of the anointing

As I write this chapter, I am reminded of the woman who anointed Jesus' feet with oil. How broken she must have felt as she kneeled down to present Christ with that very expensive gift. It has been noted by some scholars that the price of that oil today could cost as much as $1 million. I am willing to submit to you that you have to be anointed for your burial. This chapter is not for everyone. I am speaking directly to the remnant and chosen of God. You may be in a position of authority or have a lot of money but this does not mean you were anointed for the burial. *Anointed for burial* speaks to those whom God chooses to become glorified men and women for the reigning and ruling of His kingdom. If you are willing to pay the cost, then I am talking to you. How much does it cost? How high are you willing to go? It will take the oil of God to prepare you for the crucifixion that the chosen of God must face. The anointing takes place prior to you going through trials, but the demonstration of the anointing is based on what it costs you. What are you willing to pay for the gifts of God in your life? What can separate you from the love of God?

Has your ministry become your idol? Are you controlling it so tightly that even God can't get in? Is it *your* ministry or does your pastor have your itinerary? Is there any one who can tell you that you cannot go to a particular ministry engagement? If you do not have an authority in your life then I am sure that God is not the authority of your ministry. It is not your talent that has the power, but rather it is the anointing that destroys the yokes. So although you are talented for free, it will cost you to produce the glory of God.

Even Jesus Christ was submitted to John the Baptist. When Christ went to John to be baptized, God publicly announced the gift of Christ. Matthew 17:5 records God as saying, "This is my beloved son, in whom I am well pleased." No matter how talented you are, if you are not under a covering and totally submitted to authority then you are not prepared to pay the cost of the oil.

The woman who anointed Jesus' feet went through persecution and shame by the other disciples because she was a prostitute. They told her that she was not worthy to come in their presence, but Jesus thought otherwise {**JOHN 12:3**}. The disciples thought that her oil was too expensive to "waste on washing Jesus' feet", but His response welcomed her gesture as coming from a pure place of gratitude. Jesus ends the parable by saying that the he who has been forgiven much, loves him much. If God has brought you out of fornication, lust, drug addiction, or any lifestyle of sin, stop perpetrating like you were born saved. You should love and praise him much. This is called the cost of the anointing — *the oil that produces brokenness, death and resurrection.* Salvation is free, but the anointing costs. It is not on sale, discounted or marked down! You must pay the full price. How is the anointing produced? Your anointing is produced through the areas of weakness in your life. Your pains and disappointments are weaknesses that produce the strength of God. God's strength is perfected when we are weak, and it is in those times when *testing* must take place in order for God's perfection to be produced in you. Allow me to share with you my burial experience.

I attended a church where I was faithful for several years. I grew in the knowledge of the word, and I quoted the word quite frequently in every situation. I had already experienced several traumatic events in my life and piously thought that as a result of what I had been through, I was stronger now and ready to conquer anything. I served on the dance ministry for over seven years, sacrificing time away from my family to teach dance classes. I consistently fasted, prayed, and tithed, dedicated my time, committed my resources, and remained faithful over the areas where God placed me to steward. At one point I was receiving a $500.00 love offering each month, and God told me to submit my gift to the house for free. I really thought I had arrived spiritually.

I was hearing from God clearly and I knew it was God because I would have never told my self to give back a love offering. Shortly after that experience, I was brought on staff full time. I knew how to rebuke the enemy and do spiritual warfare. I was a strong prayer warrior. I told myself that this must be the third dimension. The ministry was wonderful.

Then, one day as I prepared to meet with the dance ministry, I became troubled in my spirit, and I sensed something strange in the atmosphere. This was an ordinary meeting, or so I thought. As we began to gather, I was greeted by my boss with the devastating announcement that the dance ministry was being **shut down.** Shut down? I couldn't believe what I was hearing. I asked *why,* but no explanation was given. At this point, my world collapsed. I began to question God. After all this time of serving faithfully, being dedicated and committed to the dance ministry, is the type treatment I deserve? I was confused. God, what is going on? My heart felt as if someone had taken a knife and repeatedly stabbed it. I was so hurt that I ran to my office to pack my bags. I would not answer my phone for anyone, although no one called me. When I got home I told God that I was never dancing again, never attending another church again and not to call me ever again about the ministry of dance. I told him to find another sister because I quit. I asked God if the institution called "the church" was real? Are people really saved? If it is not real, then why didn't He tell me because all those days I spent fasting I could have been eating. All I could think about was all the promises He made me and how they could never happen after this experience.

I would find myself spiraling into a deep depression and even attempted to take pills and smoke anything that could take me away from the presence of God. I was hurting and I wanted to make God feel the way that I felt, so I did not pray or speak to God for days. I was alone and I knew it. I felt as though I was nine months pregnant and someone punched their fist in my uterus to snatch out my baby. Ironically that same day I begin to bleed profusely. I told God that this was not fair because I was faithful and obedient. How could this happen to me? Side note: Who would I suggest it happen to?

I could not escape the presence of God. I began to hear His words so clearly as he reminded me of Job. Where were you when I created the moon, heavens and the stars? I then began to snap out of my depression quickly. I cried out to my Father from the depths of my soul. I told him everyone knew that the ministry was shut down except for me. The people I really loved and trusted had betrayed me. Immediately, God shared that He would demonstrate His power through all of my pain. I kept thinking *my ministry, my ministry,* and God reminded me that I was a surrogate mother. It was *His* ministry and He wanted it back. He told me to loose myself from everything. If I did not release the baby, then she would die. I cried, "God, what about everything that I purchased like the flags and banners? The things that I invested? The time that was sown? He said, "Release it all." I knew this was God because there was no way I would ever have had the strength to walk away without a fight. I am from New York City and to survive I had to learn how to fight. This fight did not make much sense to me. God reminded me that he was going to demonstrate His power through me. In agony I yielded everything to the Father — my mind, my soul, and my body to the divine will of God. I repented for everything I could even think about and I humbled myself and I died.

After several months of church people walking by me whispering, not being allowed to dance, I continued to stand. I went to church Sunday after Sunday and Wednesday after Wednesday singing songs to the Lord. I worshipped God day and night and began dancing in my living room. Everytime I pulled up to the church parking lot, I would weep. I was so embarrassed and hurt by everyone talking about me and not being able to vindicate myself or explain to others what was going on. One day God told me to sit in the front of the church and I was weeping. He said you are so concerned what these people think and you don't care about what I think. I realized that this was not about other people, but it was the cost of the anointing in my life. I want them to see you because I am preparing an audience for your resurrection. I have prepared a table for you in the presence of your enemies. God reminded me that not everyone is going to the places that He is taking me. Not everyone is willing to pay the cost. COUNT IT ALL JOY. I began to declare the word of God over my life. One day after crying on my steering wheel, the Holy Spirit reminded me that God was not moved by my tears. And immediately, the spirit of the Lord came upon me and I began to speak the word of God over my situation with power and authority.

Lesson 1: Speak the Word!

You have the authority over your situation and the angels desire to fight on your behalf. Shake off that woe is me spirit and place on the armor of God. **EPHESIANS 6:17** says that we should put on the whole armor of God! I pulled out my pebbles to slay the giants in my life. Your pebbles are not natural but spiritual. The weapons of our warfare are NOT carnal! Use your word to slay your enemies — work your word. BEHOLD, I am the head and not the tail. Who is this uncircumcised philistine that dares to defile the army of the Lord? God had shown Himself mighty before and he would do it again. I pull down every high thing that exalts itself against the knowledge of God. If you wait for others to help you, you may be waiting a long time. Encourage yourself in the Lord. I began to pray for others, knowing that God would vindicate me.

When I was finally contacted by the church, I was summoned to attend a meeting at which I was informed that there had been several allegations made against me in the church. I was totally oblivious to these allegations and vehemently refuted them. And to add further insult to injury, I was later told that the allegations were brought to the church by "my dancers." Not strangers, but my familiar friends. I realized at this point that whatever decisions were made with regard to my reinstatement, were in God's hands because I felt I had truly been "anointed for the burial." How does this story end? I'm glad you asked. For each allegation that was brought against me, I was able to produce documents to substantiate my innocence. God vindicated me and my position was reinstated.

As a result of this experience, I am much stronger and more patient now. I am reminded when Christ went to the cross he did not justify himself by declaring "I am the son of God". He did not talk about all the miracles he performed and all the people that were healed. The Bible says he mumbled not a word. In your silence, God will bring forth His judgment. If you have been persecuted for righteousness sake, I would like to recommend you read Tale of Three Kings by Gene Edwards. My spiritual mother, Dr. Aimee Kovacs, suggested this book to me and it prepared me for what I would encounter. The author writes about Saul's attempts to kill David because of his jealousy, and Absalom — the baby that he birthed — trying to kill David for his position. If Saul and Absalom are after you, be encouraged. God says he is providing an audience for His Glory!!! Don't be afraid when they catch you because you must die. "Unless a grain of wheat falls to the ground and dies, it abides alone; but if it dies, it brings forth much fruit" {**JOHN 12:24**}.

Lesson 2: Be delivered
from the bondage of people

When everyone is talking about you and lying on you, rejoice. Praise God! It only matters what God thinks about you. You do not have to change their minds. God wants to deliver you from the opinions of others. I was so concerned about what others said about me that I never considered what God said about me. God said he loves me...and you too! He said, "I know the thoughts I have for you"

{**JEREMIAH 29:11**}. This is not about others, it is about you. God wants to refine you. God wants to circumcise you. God wants to demonstrate His power through you! Humble yourself and allow the Holy Spirit to minister to you. It is not about what they say, but rather how <u>you</u> respond to what they say. God is looking at your response. Did you leave the church because they made you mad? Did you leave the ministry because they were talking about you? You have to mature and learn how to stand. If they talked about Jesus, then you know they are going to talk about you. So What!

Lesson 3: Love your enemies

God wants you to love and forgive your enemies the way that he loves and forgives you. Sometimes we pray for our enemies to be blessed, but we still hold malice in our hearts. We might say with our lips, "God help them and bless them," but in our hearts we desire them to be destroyed. Have we forgotten that man looks at the outward appearance but God looks on the heart? God really knows what your heart feels and when you have truly forgiven your enemies. If you are still gossiping about how they hurt you, how they should pay for the pain and how they are cursed for touching God's anointed, you are not dead yet. God wants to take you to a new dimension of the glorified man. Not everyone has been chosen for this high spiritual authority, so if you are going through this test, please love so that you can pass. Look at Stephen who was known as the first evangelist. When he was stoned, he had heart-felt compassion towards those who stoned him. he cried, "Forgive them for THEY KNOW not what they do." That is when you have truly died to your flesh, and you desire everyone to share the same intimacy with Christ. He realized that to be absent from the body is to be present with the Lord, and to die for Christ is to reign with Christ. His kingdom position was already secured and God was glorified even in Stephen's death. When you are able to repent for those who crucify you, a love and compassion will overtake you that supersedes your very existence. Your brokenness is parallel to your kingdom authority. There is never another time in the word of God that Christ stood up from His Kingdom seat on behalf of another as He did for Stephen {**ACTS 7:55-56**}. This battle is not yours, but it is the Lord's and he knows how to care for His people. It is His good pleasure that you become a glorified man.

Loving your enemies pushes you beyond your limitations into your destiny. If we were honest we could say that Christ had access to God the Father every day and God, being all-knowing, allowed Christ to walk with Judas. It is only those who are close to you and who you trust that can hurt you. Had Judas not been in Christ's life, who would have given him over to the Pharisees and Sadducees? Judas was assigned to Christ. It was necessary for Christ to be placed in the hands of the government to die for the sins of the world. When Christ hung on the cross, he could have dispatched angels to kill everyone, but He didn't. I know the stoning hurts but it is best for you to die willingly.

So now turn around and thank your enemies for helping you to become a glorified man.

Lesson 4: You must go to the cross alone

I was so lonely during my time of persecution that I even questioned my existence. I knew it was best for me to be alone because no one could touch my infirmities. I had two best friends and two prayer partners who were never really there when I needed them. At first their inaccessibility frustrated me because I felt I would have been there for them if they were going through, but I now know that their absence was the will of God. God knows that your well-intentioned friends can hinder your divine destiny. Look at Christ when he went to the mountains to pray before His crucifixion. He returned and His disciples were asleep. **He asked them, "Couldn't you just wait for one hour?"** When God is preparing you for the death of the old man, you must take that walk alone. People will not "get it" and they are not supposed to. This is about you and God. God has placed you on this Island of Patmos by yourself and you must gain the revelation of the glorified man. My best friends would tell me to leave the church or sue the church, but that's not God's way. If someone is trying to prevent you from going to the cross, at that point they become your enemy. I knew it was best for me to die. Jesus and the disciples were met by the soldiers that desired to kill him. Peter took out His sword and cut off the ear of one soldier and Jesus rebuked Peter and called him the enemy. If you don't go to the cross then the others that follow you won't live. You have to rebuke those who cater to your flesh, and kiss your Judas for launching you into your glorified state. That's the cost of the anointing. Are you ready to pay the price?

CHAPTER 3

The sacred

In many churches today the presence of God is not reverenced. I recently read an article about a homosexual pastor having sex on the alter when church was closed. You may be shocked by this incident; however, there are many offenses that the people inside the church commit in the Holy Place. The spirit of sexual perversion is sadistically infiltrating our pulpits, congregations, music ministries, and our youth. The sacred has been done away with as we have traded in a holy thing for entertainment and sinful pleasure. Young people are having sex inside the sanctuary while adults run, shout, jump up and down getting their Holy Ghost fix on during church service. Who is accountable for our children? We spend so much time trying to entertain them that we forget to teach them about God. Our children have no reverence or fear of the Lord.

In the Old Testament, the high priest would pray for an entire year consecrating himself before he went into the Holy, Holy place to visit the Lord. The ministers would tie bells on a rope around his ankles because they knew that if his heart was not pure before God, he would die. So if he dropped dead in the presence of a Holy God, they could not go in to get him. They would simply drag him out by the rope. It has not changed today. Most of the services that are taking place in the United States are full of dead men's bones. They are not dead physically, but they are the walking dead bearing no fruit. The world is looking and laughing at what they perceive to be a powerless church. For the most part, we {the church} are only big in our own eyes while economically and socially we are saying absolutely nothing.

We must sanctify ourselves individually and corporately at all costs so that we can present our bodies as living sacrifices. Today many mega ministries are marketing moguls and money exchangers. If Jesus turned over the tables in His day, when He returns, He will burn down entire buildings because many churches have not been dedicated to His service. A typical Sunday morning service includes a few minutes of praise and worship, the morning offering, a visitor's welcome, and, oh, don't forget the announcements! But what about the preached word? Or should I say fluff? The main entrée for most Sunday morning congregations is not the authentic word of God, but fluff and rhetoric! As a prophet of the Most High God, I declare to you today if the Body of Christ continues to play church, she will surely die.

Although we often take our sanctuaries for granted,

both in the natural and in the spiritual, there are two temple types given in the Old Testament that will shed light on the purpose and function of the temple and our worship: The Tabernacle of Moses and the Tabernacle of David.

Tabernacle of Moses

The Tabernacle of Moses is considered God's law and the prophetic call to the Body of Christ. The bible teaches us that Jesus is the fulfillment of the law. So when you hear people saying that we live only by the New Testament, they are disregarding the full manifestation and picture of the Body of Christ. The New Testament does not give you a license to sin. God has given us grace; however, if you love the Lord, then you will keep His commandments.

We know that the law alone was not good enough to keep us, so Jesus had to come on the scene to redeem us back to the Father. For the law kills but the spirit reveals. When we review the Tabernacle of Moses, we are looking at it now as a fulfillment of prophecy. It demonstrates an accurate depiction of the Body of Christ coming together. *"And He Himself gave some to be apostles, some prophets, some evangelists, and some pastors and teachers, for the equipping of the saints for the work of ministry, for the edifying of the body of Christ, till we all come to the unity of the faith and of the knowledge of the Son of God."* The tabernacle of Moses teaches us what the Body of Christ should look like and how to enter into the presence of God.

In the Old Testament, the people did more worshipping and listening to God. They would worship for hours and then bring a tape recorder to playback what the Lord had spoken {not literally, but figuratively}. If you review the Tabernacle of Moses, you will see how serious the ministers were about worshiping God and creating an atmosphere for the entrance of His presence. The tabernacle was designed in three dimensions: {1} outer court, {2} inner court and {3} the holy of holies. The tabernacle was to provide a place where God dwelled among the people. The meaning of tabernacle is *tent* and I like to think of the tent as God's covering for us. When we stay in communion and fellowship with God, he provides a covering {tent} for us. Every detail and every fiber inside the tabernacle was constructed by God's divine instruction. The High Priest managed the tabernacle and all the officers that worked in and outside of the tabernacle. Each officer was appointed and they were all from the Levitical priesthood. Not every one could handle the service of the Lord or the presence of God.

The Outer Court

The Outer Court was surrounded by white linen, which hung more than eight feet tall. There was only one entrance and it was thirty feet wide. The Levites and priests were the only ones who could enter into the *Outer Court*. As a worshipper, dance minister and praise leader, there is only one way to God. Today you represent a gate keeper for the Father and you determine who should lead worship in the sanctuary. If there are worship and praise leaders, dancers, or musicians whose lifestyles and behavior blatantly contradict the word of God, {i.e., fornication, adultery, homosexuality, and the like} it is the leader's responsibility to bring reprimand and discipline.

God is holding you responsible as a leader and their blood is on your hands. Not only that, but you are responsible for the people to whom they minister. We are spiritual beings and we minister from spirit to spirit. We should not allow someone to lead {sing, play instruments or dance} simply because he or she is anointed, but there should be a godly standard by which he or she lives and conducts him or herself. When you allow people to minister who have sin in their lives, you are in essence allowing a vile spirit to be released upon God's people. *"And he set the gatekeepers at the gates of the house of the Lord, so that no **one** who was in any **way** unclean should enter."* {2 CHRONICLES 23:19}

God has appointed you to be His eyes and ears and no man comes unto the Father unless he comes through Jesus Christ. In **JOHN 14:6,** *Jesus said **to** him, "I am **the** way, **the** truth, and **the** life. **No one comes to the Father** except through Me."* You must guard your gates and lift up the standard of the Lord at all times. If there is sin in the camp, it must be exposed! When the leader worships the Father, people should be drawn to God not to man. Guard your gates! *"I speak in human terms because of the weakness of **your flesh.** For just as you presented **your** members as slaves of uncleanness, and of lawlessness leading to more lawlessness, so now present **your** members as slaves of righteousness for holiness."* {**ROMANS 6:19**}.

In this **Outer Court,** there were two sacred objects: the "bronze altar" or altar of burnt offering; and the "laver," or washbowl. Animal sacrifices were slaughtered on the bronze altar; and the blood of those animals was shed every morning and evening as a sacrifice to God. There would be smoke and incense offered up as well. The bronze altar points to Jesus who would be that sacrifice whose blood would be shed for the forgiveness of sins. When you present yourself to the Father, sacrifices must be made.

This is not just for the Old Testament priests, but we too must make sacrifices. Jesus carried His cross and you too will have a cross to bear. No cross, no crown. Today, we should sacrifice the telephone by going on a phone fast or by shutting down e-mail. You must offer up the sacrifices of praise. You are not going to always feel like praising God, but you must make praise an act of your will. It is a sacrifice. The Tabernacle of Moses teaches us this pattern, so while you don't have to kill any lambs, you must mortify your flesh. I love the way the New Testament Greek Lexicon expresses the word mortify. It defines the term as: *to make dead, to put to death, slay, worn out, and of an impotent old man; to deprive of power, destroy the strength of.* We have to crucify our flesh before entering into God's presence. A good way to do this is to meditate on the word of God day and night and render a sacrifice of praise. Sometimes people offer up what they are feeling at the time; however, a sacrifice is giving something you love or giving out of your own need. *"**Enter into His** gates with thanksgiving, and **into His courts** with praise: be thankful unto him, and bless **His** name."* {**PSALM 100:4**} We are commanded to praise God!

He has a protocol of worship and an order for entrance. Any man that tries to enter any other way is a robber and a thief. That is why the bronze alter is the first thing you would see at the entrance of the Tabernacle of Moses. You must offer up the sacrifice of praise and if the Lord receives it then he will invite you into His holy place. As you move into the entrance, you would see the laver or washbowl where water is contained. Today the washbowl represents washing yourself in the word. The water is a cleansing process and it represents the person of the Holy Spirit. *Not by works of righteousness which we have done, but according to His mercy he saved us, by the **washing** of regeneration, and renewing of the Holy Ghost.* {**TITUS 3:5**}

The Inner Court

The Inner Court is considered the Holy Place and it contains three pieces of furniture: the table with the *consecrated bread, the lamp stand, and the altar of incense* which faced the thick curtain separating the Holy Place from the second chamber, the Most Holy Place or Holy of Holies. The bread represents Jesus being the bread of the world. *"For man shall not live by bread alone but by every word that proceeds out of the mouth of God." "I am the living bread which came down from heaven: if any man **eat of** this bread, he shall live for ever: and the bread that I will give is **my flesh,** which I will give for the life **of** the world.* {**JOHN 6:51**} You have to eat of him daily. If you are eating the word and digesting it every day then you will become more like Christ. It is impossible to be a worshipper while you're in your flesh

43

because the word of God tells us that we must worship in spirit and in truth. If you cannot eat of the bread of Jesus then you will not have life and life abundantly. Do you remember when Jesus told His disciples that I am the living Word? *"Then Jesus said unto them, Verily, verily, I say unto you, Except ye eat the flesh of the Son of man, and **drink** His **blood**, ye have no life in you"* {**JOHN 6:53**}.

This is another reason we break bread and take communion. We are constantly reminded of the bread of life. The lamp stand would light up the Holy Place, and points to Jesus the Light of the World. *Then spake Jesus again unto **them,** saying, I am **the light of the world:** he that followeth me shall not walk in darkness, but shall have t**he light of** life.* {**JOHN 8:12**}

The altar of incense is where incense is burned to release aroma to the Holy Place. It represents the intercessions going up on our behalf by the saints and our final High Priest Jesus Christ. *And the smoke of the **incense,** which came with the prayers of the saints, ascended up before God out of the angel's hand.* {**REVELATION 8:4**}

So today, as a dance minister or worship leader, you must offer up the sacrifices of praise. Wash yourself in God's word, eat of His flesh by reading and meditating on His word daily, and join the saints in intercession.

The Holy of Holies or most holy place

The Holy of Holies was the smallest, but most sacred tabernacle. Only the High Priest enters in the Holy of Holies once a year on the Day of Atonement. We thank God for Jesus!!

We no longer have to have man atone for us but we have been atoned once and for all. When Christ was resurrected the veil was torn. Now everyone has access to the father. If you pray, praise and keep His commandments you to will have access to him.

Once again the tabernacle is a replication of how we worship today. The high priest is Jesus who is constantly interceding year round on be half of the saints. The Ark of the Covenant has a covering called the mercy seat, and two cherubim carved in gold. Here the glory of God was revealed in visible form, the *Shekinah*. Because of Christ's resurrection we can go before the father and obtain grace and mercy.

In this holy place, it is invitation only. You cannot invite yourself but the King has to summon you to worship. Anyone can praise God, but not everyone lives a lifestyle of worship. Worship is about intimacy and relationship. If you come into the presence of a holy God without permission, you will surly die.

The great news is that he wants you to enter in. He has created you just for this purpose. The blood of Christ has atoned for your sins, and now you can come. Bring everything to Him, and lay it at the bronze alter. Renew your mind in His word. Cast all your cares on him through your prayers of incense, and be obedient until he invites you in to worship. Just because you are tearing up the church carpet or lying on the floor does not mean you are worshipping God. Worship is an act of the heart. I cannot tell you if you are worshipping — only God knows. I can tell you that he desires a relationship with you and if you seek him, you will find him. Encourage your dance ministry to seek God. He is no longer unavailable to you. Jesus Christ our King has given you access. Please remember there is a protocol for His glory.

The Tabernacle Of David

In the Tabernacle of David, you will find the restoration of the dance. Although dance is being embraced now in many congregations, it still carries a negative stigma in the minds of many. You will find that people look at dance either as a form of entertainment or very lustfully. It is true that dance is a powerful tool. You can use it to bring glory to God or attention to yourself. Let's take a look at John. He was beheaded because **Herodias's daughter** did a table dance for King **Herod** which swept Herod away. Okay, maybe she didn't use a table; however, when she finished dancing the King made an oath: "Ask what you will and I will give it to you". {**MATHEW 14: 8**} Already coached by her mother, she was ready: "Give me, served up on a platter, the head of John the Baptizer". This is really important because it shows you the power of the dance.

Why do you think so many music videos are parading naked women dancing? Everywhere you go you will find dance as a form of entertainment. Dance carries a spirit with it. It is probably the only thing that can transcend languages and color. You don't have to speak the same language to communicate through dance. You communicate from spirit to spirit. When you dance for God, you are truly committing your whole body as a living sacrifice, and it should be holy and acceptable. You have to use every fiber of your body to convey the message, so it is crucial that your spirit remains Holy. Because of the negative connotation of dance giving in several verses of the New Testament, dance has been kept out of the church. The enemy has used this as a ploy to stop pastors from allowing dance in their sanctuaries.

It's funny how in the Old Testament dance was a part of prophecy, celebration, travail, worship and daily activities. In the New Testament dance still exists; however, the enemy would have you believe that it does not. We read in the Tabernacle of David how the Old Testament foreshadows the New. Well, in the Old Testament when the victor returned from battle, the closest women relatives would greet him with a dance. In **JUDGES 11 :34,** Jephthah was victorious in His fight against Ammon *and returned to His house at Mizpah, there was His daughter, coming out to meet him with timbrels and dancing; and she was His only child. Besides her he had neither son nor daughter.*

1 SAMUEL 18:6 states that when David was returning from the slaughter of the Philistine, that the women had come out of all the cities of Israel, singing and **dancing,** to meet King Saul, with tambourines, with joy, and with musical instruments. This means that when Christ returns, His closest relatives will greet him with a victory dance, for he will give us garments of praise for the spirit of heaviness and turn our mourning into dancing. Hallelujah!!! This is why David's tabernacle is key. Before the Father returns, dance must be restored back to its rightful place. *"After this I will* *return and will rebuild the tabernacle of David, which has fallen down; I will rebuild its ruins, and I will set it up; So that the rest of mankind may seek the Lord, even all the Gentiles who are called by My name, says the Lord who does all these things. Known to God from eternity are all His works."* {**ACTS 15:16**} David's tabernacle was the only tabernacle that focused on the Lord's free worship. It focused on ushering in the presence of God by invoking him through dance, song, prayer and praise. This is not just for the Old Testament saints {read **ACTS 15:16**}. The Lord said he will rebuild the tabernacle of David. Why would God say this? Let's take a look at what took place in David's tabernacle.

The Tabernacle of David shows that there were really two tabernacles. One tabernacle dealt with a **kingly anointing** and one tabernacle dealt with the **priestly anointing.** The offices of the king and priest were separate in the Old Testament yet brought together in the New Testament. The kingly anointing refers to government, rule, dominion and authority, whereas the priestly anointing points to reconciliation, intercession and worship.

The first thing David did after taking Mt. Zion was to fortify it and he sought to bring the Ark of the Covenant back {**1 CHRONICLES 13**}. He set up a tent and established a new order of worship where in God was ministered to 24 hours a day {**1 CHRONICLES 15 – 17**}. After this, he then went out with His army and subdued his enemies all around. Then he gathered the spoil in order to enable the next generation {Solomon} to build the temple of the Lord {**1 CHRONICLES 18 – 22**}. That means that as worshippers, we have the ability to rule. Remember the battle does not belong to us anyway it is the Lord's. The praisers always go before the fight because it confuses the enemy. Take your rightful place as King in your house and on your job. We need more Kings like David and Jonathan.

Today, there are too many pastors sleeping with the enemy-cutting side deals with politicians to get our petitions brought before the state legislatures. If you have 20,000 people in one congregation, you can place Godly people in office. Groom your sons and daughters to lead. Just as King Solomon built the temple, so too will your children build. When David ruled as King, worship was essential to hearing from God. And David actually led worship. Where are the pastors that are not afraid to bow before a holy King? Where are the churches that are spending time corporately on their faces during Sunday service? If you are not worshipping, then tell me who you are hearing from? David ministered to the Lord freely without care of man. He was constantly seeking God for His every movement. Lord reveal your glory, the Lord is my shepherd, the Lord is my light. Please get this: you cannot worship without the Lord! David would sing prophetically and have Levites keep a record of what was said. {1 CHRONICLES 16:4} *"And he appointed some of the Levites to minister before the ark of the LORD, to commemorate, to thank, and to praise the LORD God of Israel."*

God is once again raising up the Tabernacle of David, and that includes the prophetic song. Nowhere in the New Testament or the Old Testament did He tell us to stop singing prophetically. We just did. Why? We stopped because we fulfilled the Word of God when we {the church} drove the musicians out. Before you can rebuild something, it must be torn down. The church tore it down, now God is rebuilding and restoring.

Worship leaders and dance ministers spend an enormous amount of time in rehearsals during the week and on Sunday we are so rehearsed there is no room for the Holy Spirit. I believe there are times when we should rely more on the leading of the Holy Spirit — unrehearsed and unscripted — and be free to flow whichever way He leads. You will create a song you have not heard. You will birth melodies from heaven and you will definitely do a new dance.

Another area that pleased the Lord about David was his repentance. As a worshiper you must have a pliable spirit. No one knows everything. You must come as a child to the father when trying to acquire knowledge — realizing that the Lord knows everything, and we need His wisdom in order to live move and have our being. When we make errors as worshippers, which we will, you have to quickly ask the father for forgiveness. Make repentance and forgiveness apart of your worship with the father.

CHAPTER 4

Spiritual warfare

The position of a dance minister requires one who is definitely familiar with warfare. When I grew up in the streets of New York City, it seemed like all I did was dance and fight. My mother would say, "You don't throw the first blow, but if they hit you, pick up a chair and knock them out." So I did exactly that. Little did I know that God was preparing me for spiritual warfare. **EPHESIANS 6:12** states, *"For we do not **wrestle against** flesh and blood, but **against** principalities, **against** powers, **against** the rulers of the darkness of this age, **against** spiritual hosts of wickedness in the heavenly places."* It is important to remember this: you are not fighting people, but spirits. You cannot see the spirit in the natural realm only by the spirit. Try the spirit by the spirit.

If you look at the natural location of the dance ministry in the church, you will see that we are positioned for warfare. Dancers stand in front of the congregation and in front of the pastor. They are always on the front line no matter which way you turn. Therefore as a dance minister, you must be prepared. You don't have the luxury of others to take your assignment casually or loosely. You must be girded up at all times. You never know when you will be called to minister. Saturday should not be a day of recreation for you, but rather a day of preparation. If your pastor takes time to prepare his sermon, then you should take time to prepare your dance.

Your dance should become the preached word made flesh — God's revealed voice through movement. The only way it can come from God is by quieting yourself to hear from Him. This is also apart of spiritual warfare because the enemy will do everything in his power to distract you through subtleness. Your family will visit from out of town, you'll have to take an assignment out of town, your husband will trip, and the baby won't sleep. Counteract these things through prayer. Make time to pray. Pray always. Walk and pray, shower and pray, hold the baby and pray.

The enemy knows his days are numbered and his time is short. He hates for you to dance. Dance is a reminder to him that the saints have the victory. God said that he will give you the garment of praise for that spirit of heaviness, so you must dance. Also in the Old Testament dance was used a symbol of the victor. Remember Miriam did a prophetic dance with the tambourines before Moses split the red sea, and the women dance and sang before kind David when they said *Saul has killed his thousands and David his ten thousands.* Well when Jesus returns, His closest relatives will be dancing a prophetic declaration of victory. But before Christ returns, there will be many battles to fight in spiritual warfare. The great news is that Christ left you well equipped to conquer your opponent.

The Lord has given you an armor to put on every day. As a dance minister, never leave home with out your spiritual gear. **ISAIAH 59:17** states, *"For He put on righteousness as a breastplate, and a **helmet of salvation** on His head; He put on the garments **of** vengeance for clothing, and was clad with zeal as a cloak."* Try to plead the blood over yourself, your family and your church daily.

You have the authority in your feet. Every place the soles of your feet tread upon God has given it to you. Walk in your authority. **MICAH 4:13** states, *"Arise and thresh, O daughter of Zion; for I will make your horn iron, and I will make your hooves bronze; You shall beat in pieces many peoples; I will consecrate their gain to the Lord, And their substance to the Lord of the whole earth."* Bronze hooves represent our feet as judgment. Through Christ's redemption, we are able to judge the enemy. The color brass is reddish in color signifying the serpent's throat when hissing. We will trample over the serpents throat with our feet when hissing. **LUKE 10:19** states, *"Behold I give you authority to trample on serpents and scorpions and over all the power of the enemy, and nothing by any means shall hurt you."* Walk in your authority, dance minister. You have the victory over

your finances; you have the victory over your marriage; and
you have the victory over every imagination that exalts itself
above the knowledge of God. When you are using your feet
in the dance, keep this in mind: God gave you ruler-ship in
your feet. **DEUTERONOMY 33:29** reads, *"Your enemies shall
submit to you, and you shall tread down their high places."*

Use your hands as weapons of warfare. When you are
in the congregation or in the streets ministering, you have to
know how powerful you are when you dance. When you
lift your hands, you can pull down the strong holds and
break the bondage off the people. When you lift your
hands, it tells the enemy that you have the victory and the
 saints are winning. Have you ever seen anybody cheer for a
winning team with their arms down? **EXODUS 17:11-12**
says, *"And so it was, when Moses held up his hand, that
Israel prevailed; and when he let down his hand, Amalek
prevailed.* Hands represent power and authority. *"I have
come down to deliver them out of the hand of the Egyptians,
and to bring them up from that land to a good and large
land, to a land flowing with milk and honey, to the place of
the Canaanites and the Hittites and the Amorites and the
Perizzites and the Hivites and the Jebusites."*

Clap your hands to let the spirit realm know who is in
charge. **PSALM 18:34** says, *"For God teaches our hands to
make war.* **MATTHEW 16:19** follows up with, *"And I will
give you the keys of the kingdom of heaven, and whatever
you bind **on earth** will be bound in heaven, and whatever
you **loose on earth** will be **loosed** in heaven."* Use your
hands and feet to declare war. Disturb the prince of the air.

Your hands create waves that shatter the atmosphere. Your flags and banners are the very breath of God and they breathe God's peace when you wave them. They create a yielding position in the atmosphere.

The greatest form of warfare is worship. Your obedience to God stops the enemy in his tracks. The enemy cannot touch you because he does not have jurisdiction over you. He is stopped at the gates. Lift up your banners in the sanctuary. For when the enemy comes in, like a flood, the spirit of the Lord will lift up a standard against him. Lift up your heads in the sanctuary. *"**Lift up your** heads, O you gates! And be **lifted up,** you everlasting doors! And the King of glory shall come in."* {**PSALM 24:7**}

It does not matter how powerful your gift is if you do not walk in God's obedience. Walking in His obedience yields protection for your life. Remember Jonah? He disobeyed God and was swallowed up. You will be an awesome swallowed up dancer if you do not heed the voice of the Lord. You cannot fight principalities living in sin. You must present your body as a living sacrifice. You have to mortify the members of the flesh for righteousness. **ROMANS 6:13** states, *And do not present your members as instruments of unrighteousness to sin, but present yourselves to God as being alive from the dead, and your members as instruments of righteousness to God.*

Your instruments are the members of your body, legs, arms, hands, etc. You cannot be given to drinking, fornication or lust. Many praise leaders are awesome psalmists, but their homes are a hot mess. They have the finest of everything, but no integrity. Holiness is a part of your weapons of righteousness. God is our Jehovah Nisi, the Lord our Banner. He is our God of Battle. He makes war on our behalf. When we worship him, he sends the angel Michael to do battle. You can cover the seas with your praise. You can stop bombs on territories you have never been to with a life style of obedience, submission, prayer and worship to the Most High God.

CHAPTER 5

Ministry gifts

Everyone has a gift and our gifts should be used for the edifying of the body. *"And He Himself gave some to be apostles, some prophets, some evangelists, and some pastors and teachers, for the equipping of the saints for the work of ministry, for the edifying of the body of Christ, till we all come to the unity of the faith and of the knowledge of the Son of God, to a perfect man, to the measure of the stature of the fullness of Christ."* {**EPHESIANS 4:11**} It is very important that you recognize the five-fold ministry gifts in the dance ministry. The gifts are the ministry of Christ expressed through the believer by the anointing of the Holy Spirit. That means you can have the gift and not exercise it.

Do you remember the scripture regarding the talents? Two men sowed their talents and the third man buried his. Because this man did not make use of his talent, he was cast into the lake of fire and called a slothful servant. When are you going to exercise your gift? Are you waiting on the return of Christ for the sick to be healed? Or maybe you're waiting for your pastor to heal the blind. No, perhaps you are waiting for TD Jakes to set the captive free. **LUKE 4:18** says that the spirit of the Lord God is upon you for he has anointed you to do those things. We cannot come into our fullness as a body until all the gifts are in operation. Then and only then will Christ take residence as the head of the body. If your church does not have the five-fold ministry in operation, I submit to you that Christ is not at the head. Some ministries have a great teaching ministry but they stifle the prophetic. Some ministries have a great prophetic ministry but lack apostleship and order. Until all five are in operation your ministry will suffer to some extent.

Christ is our example of the Apostle, Prophet, Evangelist, Pastor and Teacher.

Christ as Apostle
Therefore, holy brethren, partakers of the heavenly calling, consider the Apostle and High Priest of our confession, Christ Jesus. **{HEBREWS 3:1}**

Christ as Prophet
And He said to them, *"What things?"* So they said to Him, *"The things concerning Jesus of Nazareth, who was a Prophet mighty in deed and word before God and all the people.* **{LUKE 24:19}**

Christ as Evangelist

And Jesus went about all the cities and villages, teaching in their synagogues, and preaching the gospel of the kingdom, and healing every sickness and every disease among the people. {**MATHEW 9:35**}

Christ as Pastor

Shepherd the flock of God which is among you, serving as overseers, not by compulsion but willingly, not for dishonest gain but eagerly; nor as being Lords over those entrusted to you, but being examples to the flock; and when the Chief Shepherd appears, you will receive the crown of glory that does not fade away. {**1 PETER 5:2-4**}

Christ as Teacher

This man came to Jesus by night and said to Him, "Rabbi, we know that You are a teacher come from God; for no one can do these signs that You do unless God is with him." {**JOHN 3:2**}

Christ became these things to teach us how the perfected man should look. ***There is one body and one Spirit, just as you were called in one hope of your calling;*** one Lord, one faith, one baptism; one God and Father of all, who is above all, and through all, and in you all. {**EPHESIANS 4:4-6**} It is not good enough to have the gift and not use it and it is not good enough to use the gift and abuse it. You must operate in the spirit of God *"...with all lowliness and gentleness, with longsuffering, bearing with* one another in love, *3 endeavoring to keep the unity of the Spirit in the bond of peace, walking worthy of your calling in meekness and love." {**EPHESIANS 4:2-3**}* It took my ministry being shut down before I understood this principle and I am still growing in God's grace everyday.

These are all considered Spiritual Gifts — *the God-given empowered ability used for the edifying of the Body of Christ and to reveal the glory of God.* When you understand your calling, you unlock the riches of God's glory which is the inheritance of the saints. You cannot become empowered until you understand your call and operate in your gifting — not your pastor's gifting, not your mama's gifting, but **your** gifting from God. If you know you don't like to smile, why did you join the greeter's ministry? If you have a very low tolerance and become easily offended, ushering is not for you. This principle can save you a lot of turmoil and allow the ministry of the body to flow. We cannot come into the fullness of Christ with one disjointed member. *And He put all things under His feet, and gave Him to be head over all things to the church, which is His body, the fullness of Him who fills all in all.* {**EPHESIANS 1:22-23**} There are two other names for spiritual gifts: grace gift and charismata the Greek word for spiritual gifts. Spiritual gifts can be placed in three categories: *{1}* motivational gifts, *{2}* ministry gifts and *{3}* manifestation gifts. We will focus on ministry gifts to see how they apply to the dance ministry.

We mentioned earlier that your ministry gifts are the apostle, prophet, evangelist, pastor, and teacher. This group is considered your five-fold ministry. You should identify the gifts that are in your ministry and know those who labor among you. First, pray and ask God to reveal the gifts to you. Next, pray and ask God to reveal the gifts to them. Then pray and ask God to allow their gifts to be functional, pure and mature. One may have a ministry gift and operate in that gifting, but may have a negative disposition. You will always have at least one. Watch out for that "one" and be very discerning. Negativity is like a cancer that person will usually try to infect the weakest link. Before you know it, that cancer has spread through the body and the ministry is broken. The person is gifted but has the wrong spirit. Recognize the gift, but do not present the gift until it is mature. David was also gifted and he was anointed a long time before he operated in his fullness as king.

Apostle

The word Apostle comes from the Greek verb *apostello* and it means to send forth with a divine mission. You are an ambassador for the one who has commissioned you to go forth. An apostle is one who:

Plants new churches

"I planted, Apollos watered, but God gave the increase."
{1 CORINTHIANS 3:6}

Lays a foundation

"According to the grace of God which was given to me, as a wise master builder I have laid the foundation, and another builds on it. But let each one take heed how he builds on it. **{1 CORINTHIANS 3:10}**

61

Sets Order

"For this reason I left you in Crete, that you should set in order the things that are lacking, and appoint elders in every city as I commanded you. {COLOSSIANS 1:25}

The apostle has some working of all five offices and should be able to provide adequate spiritual leadership. They must also have outstanding spiritual gifts with the power and ability to establish churches. A dancing apostle will generally find themselves aiding many dance ministries and sometimes serving as spiritual mother or father. They are preachers or a teacher, or a preacher and a teacher. They tend to be the leaders in the dance ministry. People will seek you advise, wisdom and knowledge. You will find yourself helping dance ministries get started and mentoring the dance leaders. The dancing apostle loves order and you will aid the ministry in finding order. You will also help bring administration and lay biblical foundation to the ministry. Use the apostles in our ministry to go out for outside ministry engagements. If they are true they will help you build. They will also maintain order in the church if you go out. Make your apostles your assistant directors. It will free you to do more for the Kingdom.

Take particular note of the person who has the gift of apostleship but has no spiritual authority. These are the people that are always bragging about how many churches they mentor and the places they have traveled. However, if you went to their local dance ministry you might be surprised to learn of all the hell they raise. Be leery of these people. They go from ministry to ministry and church to church. Every time they are not given a platform to lead the ministry or control the minds of the people, they leave the ministry for a new gig. Try the spirit by the spirit; look for the fruit of the apostle. An apostle is a mature person. If they are operating in this office then they must have fruit.

Prophet

A **Prophet** is directed by God. They are sometimes called God's mouth piece. Prophecy can be past, present or future events that are revealed from God through the prophet. A prophet has to first be called to ministry. Just because you can prophesy does not make you a prophet. To prophesy means to one that speaketh unto men edification, exhortation and comfort. Yet there is a difference in the office of a prophet. A healing ministry and the laying of hands is a part of the prophet's office.

Prophecy can be ***predictive, directive and corrective.*** {**ACTS 21:10; ACTS 13:1-3;** and **ACTS 15:27-32,** respectively} The nature of a prophet tends to be very distant. To serve in the office as a prophet one must have two of the revelation gifts operating in their lives.

Word of wisdom — supernatural revelation by God revealing divine purpose.

Word of Knowledge — mind of God revealing things, places and people present or past.

Discerning of spirits — being able to hear and see in the spirit world.

Prophets hate unrighteousness, tend to be more direct, and often times they are loners. The prophets in the dance ministry play a key role. They will serve as visionaries and seers. They can be your greatest advocate because they can discern what the Holy Spirit wants to convey. It does not matter how wonderful your pieces or how fabulous the dance presentation is presented. If it is done out of season then it will not be received. The dancing prophets can help you with the do's and don'ts of the ministry. They will say, "Yes, do that song," and "No, don't wear that." Their concentration is the fear of the Lord. They are loners because they are spending time at home listening to the voice of God. When the word is revealed from the mouth of a true prophet, be aware — it will surely come to pass. Use your prophets to help with the choreography. Remember they are seers. Ask them about the scriptural reference for the ministry piece, the colors to wear and even the song selection.

When prophets are out of order they tend to have the Miriam syndrome. As you will remember from the Old Testament, God gave the vision to Moses, yet Miriam wanted to tell Moses how it should be done. Although this dancer may be a prophet, if God gave you the vision, then you must obey God. The Miriam syndrome tends to know everything and has a big problem with rebellion. Yes, your word is prophetic; however, you murmur so much that the leader does not even want to see you. Word of wisdom to the prophet, because Miriam talked about Moses she was struck with leprosy and died. Please leave your tongue off of God's anointed, prophet.

Evangelist

An Evangelist preaches God's good news and focuses on the lost, winning souls for Christ. John and Peter did the work of an evangelist. The assignment of the evangelist is to set the captive free. They travel outside the four walls of the church. The dancing evangelist does not like to stay in the pulpit. Glory be to God! They recognize that ministry really takes place outside the four walls of the church. If your ministry is large enough and you know some one has a heart for prison ministry or street ministry, then let them go. Please do not confine them because God desires to win souls through their dance. Use your evangelist to aid with the youth. They tend to have a special call with the non-traditional.

What you should look out for is the group that does not want to listen or get approval to dance outside the church. They are really only interested in starting their own dance ministry because they cannot be ministry leader. If you can, get them the hell out of the ministry God has birthed through you… them and the lying prophets. I am serious! Often times they will try to discredit you and misrepresent the pastor.

Pastors

The Pastors role is to feed the flock. The Greek word for Pastor is Poi which means one who cares for the sheep. The function of a pastor is to heal, strengthen, restore and pro-tect. Pastors should not beat the sheep. Pastors should not pimp the sheep. Pastors should not manipulate the sheep. Pastors should never scatter the sheep. For those that do will receive their reward.

The Dancing Preacher has a heart for the people. No matter where they go they will tend to draw a crowd. People just flock toward you for one reason or another. They also have a desire to help people and to protect people. They are very big nurturers and exhorters. Use the pastors in the dance ministry to smooth over the correction that the prophet will bring forth. They have the gift of exhortation so let them exhort and build relationships in the ministry. They will be good remembering birthdays, planning fellowships and talking about personal thing with the members. This is great to draw closeness within the ministry.

The dancing preacher can sometimes become manipulative by using their authority to beat or rule. Be very careful with this position because people will do what you say because of their respect for you.

Teachers

Teachers proclaim God's truth to bring clarity and understanding. They show you how, what, when and who. If the teaching ministry is inoperative then the people of God will perish from the lack of knowledge. **{HOSEA 4:6.}** The dancing teachers tend to be very good administratively. They love to plan, organize and give plenty of detail. They are very good administrators and they know the steps in reaching long and short term goals. Use this gift to plan outside and inside ministry engagements. They should set up the calendar. Run the dance school if you have one. Keep account of the money, put together the manuals and teach classes pertaining to dance in the word.

What to look out for is giving a teacher too much responsibility. Sometimes this gift is so needful because the visionary {Apostle} is not the person that brings forth the detail. You can rely too much on this gifting and when you turn around they are gone with the wind. You must know every aspect and detail of the ministry. Yes, you can delegate, but you don't want to wake up and say what happened. What is the seamstress' number? Who is responsible for collecting money? When are the scheduled rehearsals? What are the email addresses for the entire dance ministry? Make sure you are aware so that you may give an account at anytime.

CHAPTER 6

Ministry within a ministry

The dance minister must follow the set order of the house. You are a ministry set within the ministry. That means you should be flowing with your pastor's vision. It is very important for you to know the church's statement of belief, mission statement and where the pastor sees God taking the ministry. This will aid you in birthing choreography that is in line with the vision of the house. Because you are working with a team including the choir, praise and worship team and dance ministry, it is very important that you all look like one.

In some churches, you can see a schism because every time the leader shifts, the spirit shifts. There is no continuity. Praise and worship has a different flavor from the choir, and then the pastor will get up and everything is altered again. The Worship & Arts Ministry should be at the very pulse of what God is saying to the church. When you are finished singing and dancing, the pastor should have a greater revelation of the word of God. As a dance ministry leader, you should require the ministry to learn the church's vision statement. Sometimes the ministry should attend choir rehearsal or rehearsal with the praise team, and even fellowship together outside of the church. Make an appointment to meet with your pastor and ask him to share with you his vision for the dance ministry. What does he like? What does he dislike? This will help with the flow of the Holy Spirit and bring about a corporate anointing. Where there is unity, God commands the blessings to flow.

Make sure you submit to all authority. We serve a God that governs authority and he will not break the spiritual principle to bless you. He is a God of order, and he has ordained order and government. You may not agree with the worship leader at all times, but submit anyway. God will honor you for it. Humble yourself before the mighty hand of God, and He will exalt you in due season. Many people submit because they are not given much choice; however, you should make submission a pleasant act of your will. Because I love God, I will keep His commandments and obey those who have rule over me. It's not just the act of submission, but the posture you take when you submit. Are you always murmuring? Can you get along with the leaders over you? Do you inwardly desire them to leave or be demoted? If you feel like this, then I am willing to submit that the problem is you. Get it together. Fall on your face and worship God. When you get to that place, you will be so busy looking at yourself that you won't be able to find fault with leadership. Trust me, if it is not right, God will deal with it. You keep your eyes focused on God and watch His sovereignty. That brings me to this next section: Dealing With Yourself.

Dealing with yourself

Dealing with yourself can get ugly. *In the year King Uzziah died, I saw the Lord and he was high and lifted up.* {**ISAIAH 6:1**} You cannot see the Lord clearly until you kill everything in your mind that exalts itself against the knowledge of God. If you want to see Christ high and lifted up take some time to deal with you. Go away, quiet down and ask God to reveal you to yourself. I remember the first time I did this, I was depressed for weeks. I really thought prior to that moment that I had it going on. To my surprise, I was a filthy mess still needing the redeemer to purge and wash me from all my sins. It was not that I was committing great sins, but my thoughts were impure. I was so self-righteous and a hot mess. I looked in the mirror, and I was not pleased with what I saw.

Please, I beseech you, ask God to show you **YOU.** After crying and saying *woe is me for I am yet undone,* you will be so content that the Father loves you that you'll want to change. He only wants to shape you into the image of His son. This is a daily process by renewing your mind with God's word. God is not going to build on top of your stuff. He will tear the building down and start from scratch. That is the part that hurts the most…starting from scratch. Ouch! God's molding and shaping process can be very painful, but once the shaping is complete, you will be ready for the assignment that the Lord has prepared. When a potter begins to form his vessel of clay, he uses fire to reshape it and that which needs to be purified, requires more fire. If you are willing to endure the fire, it is worth it…for you shall come forth as pure gold.

Dealing with others

When God gives you the assignment, He does not necessarily reveal the identity of those with whom you will serve. There are several personality types you will encounter in ministry: Jonathans, Davids, Absaloms, and Sauls. Every ministry probably has one or more of these personality types within.

Jonathan

I encourage you to first seek God on who your Jonathans are. These are the people that really run the ministry, not you. They will have your back in a season of doubt. The word of God says in **MATHEW 9:37,** *"The harvest is plenteous, but the laborers are few."* Pray and ask God to bring you the laborers. God will give you the spirit of discernment which will help you to locate Jonathan. You cannot make it without him. When you locate Jonathan, love on him. He is willing to sacrifice a great deal to keep you lifted. Some of his sacrifices you will never see. They have been done in secret. Too many times, leaders take this group for granted until they lose Jonathan. He is God's gift to you so treat him well. Honor him and esteem him higher than you do yourself. Allow Jonathan to be naked in front of you, and heed his advice. He will be your eyes and ears in the ministry. Be careful when you are a ministry leader because everyone poses as Jonathan in front of you. They want to get your bags or take you to eat, but they are actually reporting on you. Watch and pray that God will show you who's who. Don't wait until adversity comes. Use your discernment now!!!

Characteristics of Jonathan:
- Comes early or on time to rehearsals
- Prays for you and with you
- Calls to check up on you
- Does not engage in idol conversation
- Helps in whatever area of service is needed {cleaning dance room, preparing garment room, creating choreography}.

It does not matter — they are there. You can trust them with money and your family secret.

David

David is an awesome person to have in the ministry. He just wants to praise God. He is not into gossiping. He is not trying to run to every convention, singles conference or new happening. He is focused on the things of God. If you give him movements to do, he will try no matter what. If you tell him you've changed rehearsal to another time, he will break his neck to get there. He can practice for hours without complaining. He just wants to remain in the presence of God. He is not interested in you or your title. He wants the presence of God. You can trust David as a ministry leader. He loves God so much that he is willing to submit wholeheartedly. David is constantly seeking and trying to please God.

Characteristics of David:
- Trained dancer or attends dance classes
- Studies the Word
- Shows up on time
- Tithes
- Follows instructions
- Assists with any area needed
- Loves people

Saul
Saul is a hot mess. He may have a higher position than you have, but this is not always the case. I am speaking of the spirit of Saul, the spirit of murder and constant use of his position of authority as a leveraging bar. You have to be careful and discerning with Saul because he will become easily intimidated. Saul has to do whatever it takes to keep His position before man. He will make you look bad to make himself look good. He shows himself as not needing anyone but inwardly he is a man pleaser. Saul has to have

the prestige, clothes and the look. Saul is going to make himself a part of the click. He will start the click. Pray that God will show you how to deal with Saul. This is not biblical, but my grandmother would say, "Feed him with a long handled spoon."

Characteristics of Saul:
- Arrogant
- Plenty of dance technique
- Haughty
- Skillful
- Loves to be seen
- Loves money and position

Absalom

I think Absalom is more dangerous than Saul in the ministry because Absalom comes from *your* womb. This is a person that you love and who you taught everything you know. You feed him, love on him, and sacrifice for him. The whole time, he is smiling in your face and stabbing you in your back. This person has low self-esteem and really wants to be you. He is very envious and jealous of you. If you can, get away from him. Do not tell him your business. Do not take him with you on ministry engagements. This person is not your friend. Inwardly, he hates you and will bring you down at every cost.

Characteristics of Absalom:
- Always complains about garments, choreography, scheduling, any changes

- Always starts confusion
- Calls others to get them to talk about you
- Always finds a way to talk to leadership about you with out coming to you
- Wants your position
- Never helps, never sacrifices
- Self consumed

Now that you are aware of the characteristics of those who will co-labor with you in ministry, use this knowledge to help you protect the gift and ministry to which God has called you.

CHAPTER 7

Starting your own dance ministry

Requirements for Starting a Dance Ministry

So you want to start a dance ministry in the church. Run now while you still have a chance! No, I'm just kidding. Dance ministry is a call, and unless the Lord has hand-picked you, you may want to consider doing something else. Dance is a strategic assignment. It is not a joke or something to play with. We are *Worshipping Warriors,* and when you want to win any kind of battle, you call the praisers.

In the Old Testament, the praisers came before the battle. Are you ready for a fight? That means that all the hell and warfare that will hit your congregation will come to you first. As soon as you say, "Here I am Lord, send me", your car will break, your spouse will start acting crazy, and it will seem like the same bills come twice a month. Anything and everything to distract you and stop you from answering your call and praising the Lord will occur. I am sure you have enough to deal with right now. Can you add the ministry of dance to your list?

Are you prepared for public scrutiny, as well interceding for your pastor and the ministry regularly? Are you ready to feel the afflictions of the saints, or to come under spiritual warfare? Can you fight for your family, church and ministry? This is an assignment not given to a wimp, but reserved for a warrior. You have to be ready! The great news is that if God gives you this assignment, then you must remember that the battle has already been won! Victory has already been given to you. *"And when he had consulted with the people, he appointed those who should sing to the Lord, and who should praise the beauty of holiness, as they went out before the army and were saying: "Praise the Lord, For His mercy endures forever." Now when they began to sing and to praise, the Lord set ambushes against the people of Ammon, Moab, and Mount Seir, who had come against Judah; and they were defeated.* {**2 CHRONICLES 20:21-22**}

Today, very little has changed with the position of a worshipper or dance minister. We are placed on the battle field on the frontline. Look at the position of your congregation. The praise dancers are on the pulpit or in the front of the church before the preacher and before the choir. That means that every fiery dart that is thrown naturally and spiritually reaches you first, and if you do not have on your whole armor, you will fall. Your victory is in your praise, and when you become a dance minister, you must increase your prayer and your praise. Moving forward, there are several areas that are crucial to your ministry.

1. You must be born again.
2. You must be submitted to a local church <u>and</u> pastor.
3. You should ask the pastor his vision toward the dance ministry, and if he would allow you to start a ministry.
4. You must fast, pray, read, and meditate on His word regularly.
5. You must be a tither.
6. You must be a worshipper — flowing in the Holy Spirit.
7. You must be an intercessor.
8. Become skillful in dance by taking lessons in dance and attending workshops regarding praise dance.

Birthing Choreography

Start praying about choreography. Many people are stuck in this area because they have never done choreography before. Listen to the song. It makes its own choreography. For example, let's use the 23rd Psalm:

> **1** *The Lord is my shepherd; I shall not want.* How does it feel for the Lord to be your Shepherd? Now close your eyes and remember when you needed him as a Father. What are you in need of? See yourself possessing that thing. Birth the movement from that place. Your expressions, body movement and thoughts should all

be geared towards not wanting for anything because the Most High God is your shepherd.

2 *He makes me to lie down in green pastures; He leads me beside the still waters.* When you think about green pastures, what mood do you feel? What do you see? Close your eyes and think about green pastures. That is the movement you created. Move your arms and show what green pastures look like.

3 *He restores my soul; He leads me in the paths of righteousness For His name's sake.* Now if you are saved, I know he has restored your soul at least one time. What did that experience feel like? Where were you when you accepted the Lord as your personal savior? What did you feel in that very moment? Were you crying? Were you laughing? Were you screaming? Whatever you were doing, go to that place and do it again.

4 *Yea, though I walk through the valley of the shadow of death, I will fear no evil; For You are with me; Your rod and Your staff, they comfort me.* Have you ever been afraid of anything? What was your greatest fear? Okay, something simple. What do you think about regularly that you cannot control? Finances, debt, fear of losing someone? See yourself overcoming that. See your bills paid. Become fearless. Now that you have overcome that fear, what does it feel like? That is the movement that should be demonstrated. Declare it in your dance. I shall not fear! Leap over fear and death.

5 *You prepare a table before me in the presence of my enemies; You anoint my head with oil; My cup runs over.* See all of your enemies in your presence when God blesses you. See yourself being anointed. What an honor! Does it make you yield to the floor? Bow in His presence. Can you see your blessings over-taking you? Does that make you joyful? Well stand up, lift your hands up, and receive His blessings.

6 *Surely goodness and mercy shall follow me All the days of my life; And I will dwell in the house of the Lord forever.* Run around the sanctuary because your friend's goodness and mercy are following you. Amen.

You just created a dance, not something you saw some-one else do but something God has done through you based on your experiences with Him.

It is essential to study to show yourself approved. Read the scriptures and learn about the dance in the New and Old Testament. Most people are familiar with David's dancing; however, dance was done by many people. A prophetic dance was done by Miriam before Moses crossed the red sea. A prophetic dance was done for King Saul when the dancers chanted, "Saul has killed his thousands and David his ten thousands". It was a custom in the Old Testament to greet the returning victor with a dance. So, as we prepare for the return of our bridegroom Jesus Christ, we need to be dancing a sign of victory for the church.

The Difference between the Secular and the Sacred Dance.

In the secular dance, one seeks to glorify him or herself based on how good their technique, skills, and abilities are; however, in the *sacred* dance, we seek to glorify God, how good he is and who he is. When you start the dance ministry, it is key to remember that it does not belong to you. It is the Father's ministry being managed by you and the Holy Spirit. It is crucial that you seek the Holy Spirit in every facet of the ministry.

CHAPTER 8

Hebrew Greek Words

There are seven basic forms of praise in the Bible. All of them involve physical activity. The following definitions are taken from the Strong's Exhaustive Concordance:

1. YADAH: Strong's 3034. **GENESIS 29:35** is the example. This is to hold out the hands. Notice that this is physical activity.

2. TOWDAH: Strong's 8426. **JOSH 7:19** is the example. An extension of the hand, i.e.{by implication} avowal, or {usually} adoration; specifically, a choir of worshippers. Notice that this is physical activity.

3. ZAMAR: Strong's 2167. **JUDGES 5:3** is the example. A primitive root [perhaps ident. with 2168 through the idea of striking with the fingers]; properly, to

wrong scripture references?!

83

touch the strings or parts of a musical instrument, i.e. play upon it; to make music, accompanied by the voice; hence to celebrate in song and music. Notice that this is physical activity — to play an instrument and sing.

4. TEPHILLAH: Strong's 8605. **PSALMS 17:1** is the example. From 6419; intercession, supplication; by implication, a hymn. Notice that this is physical activity — to sing.

5. SHABACH: Strong's 7623. **PSALMS 117:1** is the example. A primitive root; properly, to address in a loud tone, i.e. {specifically} loud. Note that this is a physical activity — shouting.

6. HALAL: Strong's 1984. **2 CHRONICLES 5:13-14** is the example. A primitive root; to be clear {orig. of sound, but usually of color}; to shine; hence, to make a show, to boast; and thus to be {clamorously} foolish; to rave; causatively, to celebrate; also to stultify: {stultify is to make appear foolish or ridiculous.} Notice that this is physical activity. This one is the "go for it" abandonment in praise. It is what they did when the glory cloud filled the house so that none could stand to minister.

7. TEHILLAH: Strong's 8416. **PSALMS 22:3** is the example. From 1984; laudation; specifically {concretely} a hymn. Notice this is physical activity. A hymn — singing; which is physical.

These are the seven basic forms of praise in the Bible. ALL ARE PHYSICAL ACTIVITY. Worship is spiritual, not physical. One can praise and worship at the same time. One can praise without worshipping and one can worship without praising. We have redefined praise and called it worship in the church today with regard to singing and playing music. There is no definition of worship in the Bible that suggests it involves music. Worship is a spiritual thing.

Worship is "proskuneo" in the New Testament. It is derived from two words "pros" and "koun". "Pros" means toward. "In the beginning was the Word and the Word was with God". This word "with" is "pros", meaning *toward.* "Koun" means *dog.* What is this, *toward dog?* Toward GOD. That is what the Word {Jesus} is. We should be toward God, like Jesus is; but what about the "koun" part? Dog? This doesn't make sense unless you look at the attributes of a dog. Dog is called man's best friend. A dog is loyal, obedient and trusting. If old Shep is lying in the corner asleep and you call his name, he will immediately turn his eyes and attention to you, ready for any command you may give him. We need to be like these words "toward" and "dog". We need to have our lives, our everything, toward God. We need to have the attributes of loyalty and obedience — a setting of our hearts to please our master.

You could say then that worship is a spiritual positioning or relationship with God. It is placing Him on the throne instead of us. It is recognizing Him as Lord and Master and acting accordingly. *"Then those who were in the boat came and worshiped Him, saying, "Truly You are the Son of God."*

{**MATT 14:33**} Notice here that they did not play a song. They did not tap out a beat with the oars nor did they sing. They did not fall down. It says "they came and worshipped {proskuneo} Him." They simply said "truly You are the Son of God." This clearly says it. Worship is a spiritual positioning.

Praise is a physical activity. The song we sing and accompany with instruments is praise. The word for it is *zamar* {as defined above}. We can proskuneo while we zamar, but zamar is not proskuneo. The reason I put so much emphasis on this is that if we say music and songs are worship, then we get into quality comparison. Does the better musician worship better? If music is worship, can we begin to worship music? I think this is an area in which we need to be careful.

Take a look at the word Tehillah . This is a hymn. We will take a look at what a hymn is. First, I would like to point out that God inhabits Tehillah. *"But You are holy, enthroned in the praises of Israel."* {**PSALM 22:3**} The word praise in this verse is "Tehillah". This is the ONLY verse in the Bible that says God inhabits the praises of His people. Do not mis-understand me. He responds to all forms of praise, but He inhabits Tehillah. I am not saying He can't inhabit the others. I am saying the Word does not say that He does.

So why does God choose to inhabit a hymn? Let's go to the New Testament and define what a hymn is since the word does not occur in the Old Testament. *"And do not be drunk with wine, in which is dissipation; but be filled with the Spirit, speaking to one another in psalms and hymns and spiritual songs, singing and making melody in your heart to the Lord."* {**EPHESIANS 5:18-19**}

We see here that there are three types of songs that we are to sing when we assemble. Let's define them and understand what they are. First, what is a psalm? Per the Strong's Concordance: *5568 psalmos {psal-mos'}; from 5567; a set piece of music, i.e. a sacred ode {accompanied with the voice, harp or other instrument; a "psalm"};* collectively, the book of the Psalms.

A set piece of music. That means it has been recorded and is reproducible. Don't we have hymn books? Aren't they "set music"? Could it be that we have altered another definition?

A hymn then must be different than a psalm. By definition then, a hymn is: *5215 humnos {hoom'-nos}; apparently from a simpler {obsolete} form of hudeo {to celebrate; probably akin to 103; compare 5667}; a "hymn" or religious ode {one of the Psalms}.* Comparing the two words, we see that both are odes.

What is an ode? *5603 oide {o-day'}; from 103; a chant or "ode" {the general term for any words sung; while 5215 denotes especially a religious metrical composition, and 5568 still more specifically, a Hebrew cantillation}. Any words sung.* Both the psalm and the hymn are "any words sung". Notice in the above definition of ode, any words sung is in contrast to metrical composition or Hebrew cantillation. What I'm getting at is this: A psalm is a set piece of music and since an ode is any words sung {common to both psalm and hymn} then a hymn must be other than set music which would be spontaneous. Any spontaneous words sung is a hymn. Once a hymn is set down and recorded, it then becomes a psalm. Our hymn books are really *psalm books*. They are hymns {spontaneous} that have been recorded — hence they become psalms.

Look at the verse again "spontaneous song, recorded songs and spiritual songs". Doesn't this make more sense? Notice the word tehillah is derived from halal. This means that the hymn {tehillah} has the flavor of halal. So then we have tehillah which is a spontaneous song which has the flavor of halal. It means 'go for it' singing to God from the heart. God inhabits this. Why? God is creative and spontaneous song is creative. Need I say more? Why am I dwelling on this so heavily? Take a look at spiritual songs. What are they? A spiritual song is "ode pneumatikos". We already know ode is any words sung.

What is *pneumatikos? 4152 pneumatikos {pnyoo-mat-ik-os'}; from 4151; non-carnal, i.e. {humanly} ethereal {as opposed to gross}, or {daemoniacally} a spirit {concretely}, or {divinely} supernatural, regenerate, religious: KJV— spiritual.* Compare 5591. Spiritual. Any words that are spiritual. This would be from God; the song of the Lord. If the words are from God, then they are prophetic. So we are to sing spontaneous songs, recorded songs and prophetic songs.

This raises the question, "How can I sing prophetically if I am not a prophet"? Paul says that he would have us ALL prophesy. That means all, including YOU. Therefore it is within our grasp. Jesus lives in you, correct? Jesus is THE Prophet. If He is in you, then He can prophesy through you. Therefore open your mouth and it will happen, if you let Him.

Look at this idea: Since God inhabits Tehillah, if you sing spontaneously, He lives in every word. Since He is living in every word, if you yield to Him, it is Him singing. Hence you are now singing the prophetic song. All a prophet does is speak the words God gives. What is the difference if it is sung? None. In fact if you search a little, you will find that the book of Psalms contains many prophetic songs. You will also find prophetic songs outside of the book of Psalms. Consider this: The Book of Psalms is the "Book of Tehillalum". Tehillalum is plural for tehillah.

CHAPTER 9

Ancillary

In creating a ministry piece, the first step you want to take is to seek the Father. Any time you are ministering before people, you want to ask daddy what you should do. See, he already knows who will be there and what their needs are. He knows if they are dealing with physical and emotional abuse. He knows if they are jobless and friendless, and He knows if they have not accepted Him as their personal savior. You will find some people that take one dance and use it for all occasions; however, that is not effective. What will minister to a group of elderly women in a nursing home may not minister to a group of men in a prison.

Each place you enter carries a different assignment. Each territory comes with different spirits. A home going celebration is different from a wedding. You will find tremendous grief at home goings. The spirit of mourning is generally in the atmosphere. You want to consider two primary factors: God's purpose for you being there and the dance. Your dance should bring forth joy, peace, assurance and conviction in that place. For those who are visiting, that service may be the only church they see, so at that point you become the pastor. You should witness through your dance. Find out the logistics: What is the age group? Who are the people? What is their ethnic background? What is the purpose of the event?

A Sunday service is different from prison ministry. In a men's prison, you will see so many strong holds that are evident: the spirit of greed, pride and lust to name a few. So you do not want to select a song that goes right into worship without expounding upon the word or speaking to their situation. Remember, God meets us where we are, and you were not in the throne room on your first day of salvation. Many times you were in a pit and gutter and at your last point screaming, "I need you Lord". That is when the Lord picked you up and drew you from that place. So, minister from that place. It is no different with the prisoners. You may not have been locked up behind bars, but your mind was captive and you had to have strongholds broken over your life, blood line and generation. Your ultimate goal is to bring forth salvation through your dance. Luke 4:18 states, "The spirit of the Lord God is upon you for he has anointed you to preach to the poor and to set the captive free". You are not going to your dance engagements as a dancer, but rather as a minister of the gospel.

Logistics

Once you have the logistics down concerning where you will be ministering, consider the season that the body of Christ is in on the liturgical calendar. This only applies to ministry inside the four walls. If you are at a hospital, prison, or shopping mall, people may not be familiar with your customs or traditions. This applies to sanctuary ministry. If it is Resurrection, Christmas, Communion or a celebration that is hosted each year in your church, be mindful of the service protocol. You don't want to display the birth of Christ during Communion. Your dance must be relevant to where the people are. They will be in the frame of mind concerning Christmas, so deal with Christ's birth through your dance. It can also mean the people are birthing something new. Get a calendar and write down the things that take place in your church every year. Now, set a timeline for yourself — a time of consecration. Use this time to prepare and ask the Father what he would have you do during this liturgical season. Read the word concerning that time so that it may also bring you illumination and knowledge.

Okay you have the logistics, you have the season, and now you need a song.

Song selection

When selecting music or songs, please do not choose them based on the Top 20 on the Billboard Chart. Find music that ministers to you. Find a song that speaks to your heart and then go into worship in your house. Generally, if the song touches your spirit and brings you into worship, then it will bless the people. You can only minister from your spirit because we worship in spirit and in truth. Therefore, you may be drawn to a very popular song, but if it does not speak to the heart, continue to pray and seek God concerning your song. God is birthing a new song in your belly, so sometimes you will find yourself creating your own music and writing things you have never heard on the radio. Don't be afraid to explore. *"He has put a new song in my mouth; Praise to our God; Many will see it and fear, And will trust in the Lord."*

You keep telling yourself you are not a singer; however, you are a worshipper, so a song must come from your spirit. Go to that deep place. Take time with the Father every day and I guarantee you songs, dance, and vision will be birthed. When you have the music, let your dance marry the song. That means that if the psalmist is talking about lying down in the presence of the Lord, then you should not be leaping during that part of the song. You should be in tune with what the psalmist is singing.

In dealing with the youth, you want to meet them where they are and not become one of the secular artists they watch on MTV. Too many times in congregations you will see youth leaders and pastors trying to reach the youth by playing the most popular secular artist in the sanctuary during their games, outings, conferences or even church services. Remember, the sanctuary is a holy place and it should not be perverted with the lust of the world and money exchangers. You DO NOT have to succumb to popular music. The youth don't need a cool DJ and a rock song to be excited about attending church. Keep *the main thing* the main thing. You are a caregiver who watches over their souls. If you we were meant to entertain them, then the church would be a night club. If you want to save them, then pray and ask God how you may best reach the youth. Remember, the word of God tells us that if we lift Him up, HE will draw all men unto himself. Well that includes the youth too. Try lifting up the name of Jesus and watch the youth come to Christ.

Once you select your music, it's time to choose a garment.

Garments

When God gives you the song and choreography, He will also give you vision concerning garments and pageantry. Often times you will not see these items in a dance store. Remember, in the body of Christ we do not have costumes. *Costume* is a term used in the secular arena for plays, recitals, etc. In the Old Testament, when God gave instructions to Aaron concerning garments, He was very detailed and specific. He talked about the colors, dimensions, tailor and fabric. We serve an excellent God full of detail and when he is specific about certain things, I think they have a great deal of relevance to the body of Christ. Through the book of Exodus, the word repeats *consecrate your garments that you may minister to me as priests.* You are an ambassador of the Most High God and a part of a royal priesthood. So please stop buying the first thing you see in a dance shop. Often times, those pieces are created by people who don't have an understanding of holy garments; therefore, the quality of the garment does not exist. Sometimes the garment is too reveal-ing, too short, or see-through. You are a Priest, so dress like it!

If you were to reflect upon the scriptures you will remember the lady with the issue of blood. Once she touched the hem of Christ's garment, virtue left His body and she was made whole. Your garments are a sacred part of the ministry and they should be given a great deal of prayer and thought. Your garments are holy. Here is what the Lord instructed the Levites to do concerning their gar-ments in **EXODUS 28:1-2:**

> *"Now take Aaron your brother, and His sons with him, from among the children of Israel, that he may minister to Me as priest, Aaron and Aaron's sons: Nadab, Abihu, Eleazar, and Ithamar. And you shall make holy* **garments** *for Aaron your brother, for glory and for beauty."*

In the Old Testament, you could identify the Levites by the robes they wore. They were not like everyone else, but they represented the priesthood. Even today in many con-gregations you will see the bishops, elder and ministers in a different robe from the lay people. Well, news flash! You are a minister and you should wear appropriate attire that reflects whose you are and who He is. Represent the father in the beauty of His holiness. *"Then you shall take the gar-ments, put the tunic on Aaron, and the robe of the ephod, the ephod, and the breastplate, and gird him with the intricate-ly woven band of the ephod. You shall put the turban on His head, and put the holy crown on the turban. And you shall*

*take the anointing oil, pour it on His head, and anoint him.
Then you shall bring His sons and put tunics on them. And
you shall gird them with sashes, Aaron and His sons, and
put the hats on them. The priesthood shall be theirs for a per-
petual statute. So you shall consecrate Aaron and His son.*
{**EXODUS 5:29 5**} God gave Aaron instructions concerning
His garments. They should only be worn in certain places.

Your garments should not be worn outside in the
church parking lot. Your garments should not be worn out
to eat after you have ministered but they are holy garments
and should be worn for ministry to the Lord. Take care of
your garments. Wash your body before you put them on.
They should not be thrown at the bottom of your closet, nor
left in the trunk of your car. You should never throw your
garments in a bag because they are holy garments.

Pray about an anointed seamstress. You'll want someone you can sit with and share the revelation God has given
you, someone who will pray before and after making your
garments. Once your garment is complete, anoint yourself in
your garment. **EXODUS 29:29** states, *"And the holy garments
of Aaron shall be His sons 'after him, to be anointed in them
and to be consecrated in them."* It also mentions who should
wear the garments and where they should wear them.

In a prison, men deal with issues of lust, so you don't
want to wear your pretty sanctuary garments because it may
distract them. Instead of thinking about salvation, they will
be thinking about you. All the focus should be on God. So
you need to pray about the logistics of the venue so that you
may be wise in reaching the people.

Colors

When you are considering your colors, think about the purpose of your dance, and then reflect on the song. Is the musical selection a processional, prosperity or resurrection service, or are you speaking about grief and sadness? There are colors that reflect each of these moods. Listed below, I detail some colors and the scriptural references. Please use the scriptures to determine the color of your garments.

Color	Meaning	Scripture Reference
Red	Blood and atonement	LEVITICUS 17:11; HEBREWS 9:12-14
Blue	Heaven and heavenly grace	EXODUS 24:10
Purple	Royalty	JUDGES 8:26; MARK 15:17-18
White	Purity and holiness	PSALM 51:7; MATTHEW 17:2; REVELATION 3:4
Silver	Redemption	NUMBERS 18:15-16
Gold	Divinity and God's Glory	EXODUS 37, EXODUS 40:34-35, REVELATION 1:13-14
Bronze/ Brass	Judgment	EXODUS 27:1-3; EXODUS 30:17-21
Yellow	Celebration and joy	ISAIAH 51:11; ISAIAH 61:3; HEBREWS 1:9
Green	New life	PSALM 92:12-14; HOSEA 14:8
Brown/ Grey	Repentance and humility	ESTHER 4:3; DANIEL 9;3-5
Orange/ Yellow/Red	Fire and the Holy Spirit	ACTS 2:3
Plum	Richness, abundance, infilling of the Holy Spirit	HOSEA 2:22; JOEL 2:24
Black	Sin and death	PSALM 23:4; EPHESIANS 5:11

Banners And Flags

In churches today, there needs to be a greater understanding of flags and banners. You will find the people with the least technique carrying the banner because it is much easier to do that instead of learning choreography. The banners mean so much more than that, and if we really understood the relevance no matter how skilled you are, we would all want to pick up a banner.

Banners are a symbol of solidarity, unity and the oneness of God joining the body of Christ. Banners reflect this unity. In Israel, they would use fabric to bring a group of people together to give vision and direction. When a banner is raised, it declares victory. In Israel, there was no email or telephones. Drums were used to give commands, and banners were used as a form of communicating messages. The flag denoted where the King resided, as well as the victor in battle. The flag barriers had no weapons. Their oath of loyalty had to be solid. They would rather die than lose the flag. The person who held up the flag kept the courage and hope for the entire army. The Church is God's army, and we must lift up His standard in the earth, which is why the use of the banner in dance is so vitally important.

Reprimand

If you are *sat down* {a church-imposed leave or absence} at your church by your Pastor, then your garments should be taken and given away. Yes, you read correctly. I know you were rolling with me until I said that because many people get sat down but they keep doing ministry. SIT DOWN. Let the Lord restore you. Start again. Your garments should be given to those whom the Lord has ordained to do ministry during that time. When He restores you, He will give you a new garment of praise for your spirit of heaviness. When Aaron was sat down, he was derobbed. {**NUMBERS 20:25-27 25**} *"Take Aaron and Eleazar His son, and bring them up to Mount Hor; and strip Aaron of His garments and put them on Eleazar His son; for Aaron shall be gathered to His people and die there."*

Stop playing games with the ministry. It is sacred. It is a holy thing. There are too many very popular singers and dancers parading around in sin — changing husbands like a dance skirt, men sleeping with men. Not only will you be sat down, but you will surely DIE.

About
the author

SABRINA MCKENZIE is a trained dancer with 18 years of experience, that includes dancing for various artists in the music industry. Mrs. McKenzie trained at St. Benedict School of Dance in New York City and has danced with Springfield Academy, Wings of Faith dance team and Born Again Dance Ministry.

This Morris Brown College graduate is currently the Director of the "New Birth Liturgical Dance Ministry" under the leadership of Bishop Eddie L. Long, Senior Pastor of New Birth Missionary Baptist Church. She oversees 150 dancers and several dance ministries which include Praise & Worship, Born Again, (Men) Lamb Of God Worshippers and the Children's dance ministry.

As a professional dancer, Sabrina is the overseer and choreographer for the Gospel Heritage Foundation dance ministry segment. Her dance and choreography repertoire include choreography for the Gospel Heritage Conference, Dottie Peoples Live video, Gospel Dream which aired on BET, NBA all star weekend and the Evander Holyfield heavy-weight championship. Additionally, Sabrina was featured as a solo rap artist on Bishop Eddie L Long's CD release titled "Those Who Are Not Prepared Will Not Survive."

As a community activist, Sabrina is very involved with innovative program development for inner city youth. Sabrina McKenzie believes that the Greatest Leader is the best Servant.

For registration or vendor

information, please visit

www.sabrinamckenzie.com

or call 678-754-2662

*For conference details
and booking information for
Sabrina McKenzie Ministries
call 678-754-2662*

(JEREMIAH 29:8–14)

¹¹ For I know the thoughts that I think toward you, says the Lord, thoughts of peace and not of evil, to give you a future and a hope. ¹² Then you will call upon Me and go and pray to Me, and I will listen to you. ¹³ And you will seek Me and find Me, when you search for Me with all your heart.

You can live a lifestyle of worship & holiness. You can make it. You can put off the old man. You can live with a renewed mind. Your trials have made you stronger, wiser and more patient. Do not be in fear — launch out into the deep. Don't look at the faces of men, and don't put your trust in your finances, but instead you must trust the Most High God. He can keep you and provide for you.

As an Apostle of the Most High God, I Decree this prayer over you: I speak the oracles of my Daddy Jesus the Christ that You can do ALL things. You are the righteousness of God. You are not of this world. You are an ambassador of the Kingdom of God. I stand as a spiritual sniper and shoot down every weapon designed to kill, steal and destroy the plan of God for your life. I stand as a gate keeper and spiritual cheerleader celebrating your victory. I assassinate the past hurts of molestation, rejection, physical, verbal and spiritual abuse. Place your hands on your belly:

I speak to your spirit and I say be free!!!!!!!!!!! I break every generational curse that will try to hold you. I bind the spirit of mind control that will try and grip you. You are free! I speak crop failure to the spirit of religion that will try to control you. You are free!!!

I loose love and obedience to God in your atmosphere. I launch your angels to the North, South, East and West to cover and protect you. I loose the favor of God over you. I plead the Blood of JESUS over you. Place on your armor, soldier.

(EPHESIANS 6:13–18)

¹³ Therefore take up the whole armor of God, that you may be able to withstand in the evil day, and having done all, to stand. ¹⁴ Stand therefore, having girded your waist with truth, having put on the breastplate of righteousness, ¹⁵ and having shod your feet with the preparation of the gospel of peace; ¹⁶ above all, taking the shield of faith with which you will be able to quench all the fiery darts of the wicked one. ¹⁷ And take the helmet of salvation, and the sword of the Spirit, which is the word of God; ¹⁸ praying always with all prayer and supplication in the Spirit, being watchful to this end with all perseverance and supplication for all the saints.

I pronounce the blessings of Abraham, Jabez and Solomon over your life. You are loosed to dance, to live, and to be FREE!!!!!!!!!